Butterflies
to Colour

Illustrated by Jenny Cooper

Designed by Nelupa Hussain
Written by Megan Cullis

D0452754

This book also includes
some moths.

Moths are related to
butterflies, but unlike most
butterflies, many of
them fly at night.

Malachites

Pronounced 'mal-a-kite', malachites are named for a brilliant green gemstone.

Lots of malachites live in mango, citrus and avocado orchards in Florida. They feed on overripe fruit.

Olive green and brown undersides

Mango

Malachites also feed on flower nectar, bat dung and even dead animals.

Monarchs

Monarch butterflies are sometimes known as 'Wanderers' because they can fly very long distances.

Every August in North America, millions of monarchs fly thousands of miles south, in search of warmer weather.

Female monarchs have darker veins on their wings.

Their bright orange and black wings warn birds that they are poisonous to eat.

Males have a black spot on each hind wing. These release special chemicals to attract a female.

Peacocks

Peacock butterflies have bright spots on their wings, a little like the spots on a peacock's tail.

If the butterfly is disturbed, it makes a hissing noise by rubbing its wings together.

The spots look like the eyes of a bigger animal. These frighten the enemy away.

Sooty brown undersides

In winter, the butterflies hide in hollow tree trunks. Their undersides blend in and keep them hidden.

Moroccan orange tips

These small, delicate butterflies are usually found in Morocco, in North Africa.

Males

Their orange wing tips warn enemies, such as mice and birds, that they are unpleasant to eat.

Female orange tips have pale yellow and green undersides. Their uppersides are mainly white.

When the butterflies close their wings and cover their orange tips, their mottled undersides keep them hidden among the flowers.

Five-bar swordtails

Five-bar swordtails live in the rainforests of South Asia. They often gather along streams and river banks.

Their long tails look like swords pointing in the air. These make them look bigger and more frightening to their enemies.

Black stripes, or 'bars', on each forewing

Tongue

These male swordtails are using their long tongues to drink salts and other minerals from the muddy ground. This is known as 'mud puddling'.

Queen Alexandra's birdwings

Queen Alexandra's birdwings are the biggest butterflies in the world, with wingspans as wide as dinner plates.

They are very rare, and can only be found in the rainforests of Papua New Guinea.

Their dazzling green and blue wings warn other animals that they are poisonous to eat.

Bright yellow, poisonous body

These are male birdwings. They are fierce enough and big enough to chase away small birds.

Eighty-eights

Eighty-eights get their name from the black and blue patterns on the underside of their wings, which look a bit like the number 88.

There are around 40 different kinds of eighty-eights. They all live in the tropical rainforests of Central and South America.

Number 8

Underside

These eighty-eights are feeding on the fruit of a tropical plant, called guarana.

Males have patches of purple sheen on their uppersides.

Swallowtails

Swallowtails get their name from the pair of tails on their back wings, which look a little like a swallow's tail.

Sometimes, hungry birds snap at their tails and pull them off...

They keep their wings beating almost all the time, even when they're feeding.

...but the swallowtail can escape and live without its tail.

Tail

The red spots on the hind wings are called eyespots.

They draw the enemy's attention away from the butterfly's body, so it doesn't get hurt.

Purple-shot coppers

Many purple-shot coppers live in the mountains of Southern Europe, Africa and Mongolia.

Parts of the males' gleaming coppery wings glow purplish in the sunlight.

As they fly, their wings flash purple, which helps to confuse their enemies.

Female underside

The females' coppery wings are speckled with lots of big black spots.

Blackberry flowers

Male

Female

Lesser purple emperors

Lesser purple emperors drink honeydew – a sweet, sticky liquid often found on plant leaves.

Their wings are mainly orangey-brown. But, in the sunlight, the males' uppersides shine deep purple.

Males also feed on the salts and minerals found in road tar, car fumes and even human sweat.

Male

Female

Southern festoons

Many Southern festoons live in the hot, dry vineyards of France and Italy.

They get their name from the zig-zag patterns on their wings, which look a little like hanging decorations known as festoons.

Bright flashes of red on their wings warn enemies away.

As they fly, the patterns on their wings look blurred. This makes it difficult for enemies to spot them.

Marsh fritillaries

Marsh fritillaries are usually found in boggy grassland. They are becoming very rare in Europe, because their homes are being turned into farmland.

Their orange and yellow checkered wings look a little like stained glass windows.

As they grow older, the patterns on their wings fade in the sun.

Buttercup

Marsh fritillaries' wings sometimes look shiny, which is why they are also known as 'greasy' fritillaries.

Io moths

Pronounced "eye-oh", Io moths live in the forests of North America.

Male Io moths have feathery antennae.

A moth's antennae are usually thicker than a butterfly's.

Like most moths, and unlike butterflies, they only fly at night.

Female

Like many moths, Io moths have fat, hairy bodies.

If an enemy attacks, the moths reveal their wing spots. The spots look like an owl's eyes, and frighten enemies away.

Atlas moths

Atlas moths get their name from the patterns on their wings which look a little like maps. They live in the rainforests of Southeast Asia.

Atlas moths are the biggest moths in the world — bigger than many birds.

Each hooked forewing looks a little like a snake's head. This scares off other animals.

This huge, spiked caterpillar will develop into an atlas moth.

Black mark looks like a snake's eye.

These triangular parts are see-through. No one knows why.

Madagascan sunset moths

Known as "noble spirits", these moths live in the rainforests of Madagascar, off the coast of Africa.

They get their name from the rich reds, oranges, yellows and blues of a setting African sun.

Sunset moths feed on the nectar of white flowers, such as this tea plant.

Sometimes they are mistaken for butterflies, because they fly during the day unlike most other moths.

The shimmery metallic patterns warn enemies that they are poisonous to eat.

Colouring hints and tips

You can use coloured pencils, felt-tip pens, or watercolour paints or pencils to colour in your pictures. If you use watercolours, put some card under your page to stop the rest of the book getting wet.

Coloured pencils

Coloured pencils give a soft effect and are good for doing shading.

To fill in large areas, do lots of lines all going in the same direction.

In areas with shading, press firmly for the dark areas, then gradually reduce the pressure where the colour gets lighter.

You can blend different colours together by shading them on top of each other.

Watercolours

Make watercolours lighter by adding more water, or darker by adding less.

For distinct colours, let one colour dry before you add the next.

Wet watercolours blur together.

Shading in dark areas

When you're colouring in, you'll find some areas covered with faint dots. These show you where to fill in with black or dark brown or purple.

With thanks to Matthew Oates, National Trust
Digital manipulation by Nick Wakeford

First published in 2011 by Usborne Publishing Ltd, Usborne House, 83-85 Saffron Hill, London EC1N 8RT, England. www.usborne.com
Copyright © 2011 Usborne Publishing Ltd. The name Usborne and the devices ⚲ 🌐 are Trade Marks of Usborne Publishing Ltd. All rights reserved. No part of this publication may be reproduced, stored in a retrieval system, or transmitted by any means, electronic, mechanical, photocopying, recording or otherwise, without the prior permission of the publisher. UKE. Printed in Dongguan, Guangdong, China.